MW01010308

Freaking Idiots Guide to Selling on eBay

How anyone can make $100 or more everyday
selling on eBay …

FREAKING IDIOTS GUIDES

By Nick Vulich
Copyright 2012

Table of Contents

Thank you for purchasing this book. **Freaking Idiots Guides to Selling on eBay** is an attempt to bring you easy to implement solutions for common eBay selling problems. If you found the contents helpful, please consider taking a few minutes to leave a review on Amazon.

Just as feedback helps eBay buyers decide whether to purchase from you or from someone else, Amazon Reviews help Kindle Book buyers chose which books may work best for them. If this book helped you please consider leaving a five star review. Other readers will appreciate your advice, and I will appreciate the extra customers your endorsement brings me.

If you have any comments or questions, feel free to contact me at nick@digitalhistoryproject.com. Any corrections will be addressed in future editions.

If You Don't Read Anything Else – Read This

If I could give potential eBay sellers any advice, it would be to start out slow.

Take the time to really get a feel for eBay.

To be a good seller, you really need to buy a few items first. You need to know what it's like to search eBay, trying to find the item you're looking for. You need to feel the thrill of winning a closely followed auction. You need to feel the disappointment of being outbid in the last few seconds of an auction you were winning all along.

There's a certain amount of anticipation that builds up waiting for that new book or game or pair of jeans to arrive.

You need to check out the packaging when your item is delivered.

What kind of appearance does the box or mailer make? Does it live up to your expectations? Hopefully it's not smashed, or the corners aren't dinged. Mailmen can be rough on your item.

If you haven't experienced the thrill of winning an auction, or the excitement of unpacking your new treasure, you are going to have trouble selling on eBay.

To be an eBay seller, you need to be an eBay buyer.

Introduction

Are you wondering how you can make a few hundred bucks fast, without hitting the streets? Would you like to know how you can put $100 in your hands, whenever you're running a little short on funds? Would you like to have your own personal money machine?

This book can help you with all of these things.

What you are about to learn is how to make $100 everyday selling on eBay.

Unlike many other books you may have read, this book is going to be short, and to the point. After all, you're anxious to put everything in motion, so we are going to take several short, simple, baby steps to move you in the right direction.

What I'm going to give you is a plan that you can follow over and over again, to make money now – and in the future, whenever you find yourself strapped for a little cash.

***

First let me tell you what this isn't. It's not a get rich quick scheme, where you can put in fifteen minutes, and have $1000 in your mailbox the next morning. It's more like a job, with lots of overtime, and hard work. But, if you follow the plan –

I can promise that you will have an extra $100 in your pocket whenever you need it …

Why Me?

 What makes me qualified to tell you how to sell on eBay?

My name is Nick Vulich. I have been selling on eBay since 1999. Last month I sold over 300 old magazines that most people and libraries would just throw away as worthless junk. In my better months before the recession hit back in 2008, I used to take in $5000, even $6000 a month.

According to eBay I have completed 29,260 transactions since November 2, 2001, for a total of $397,252.88, and that's just on my history-bytes id.

I think that makes me uniquely qualified to show you how to make a few bucks on eBay. I know what it's like starting out, and trying to figure out just what it is you want to sell, and that's not anything – compared to trying to figure out how you're going to approach selling those same items.

It's scary. And, it's that fear that keeps a lot of people from even trying to sell on eBay. I don't know how many times I have shown people what I do, and they say – yeah! They understand. But, they don't get it, because they don't understand why people buy what I sell.

My point is, I know the ins and outs of eBay, and if you are ready I can show you what you need to know to help you take that next step, where you can make $100 TODAY, and every day that you need it.

Getting started

eBay Account. The first thing you're going to need is an eBay account.

The good news is – They're free, and you can sign up for one in less than five minutes. If you don't already have an eBay account you can sign up for one now by visiting get started with eBay.

When you go to sign up they're going to ask for some simple information. They will need to know your name and email address. Next they're going to ask you for a user name. This is how people will come to know you on eBay, so be sure to put some thought into it. If you know what you want to sell, it will make it easier.

I sell historical paper and ephemera, so my eBay moniker is history-bytes. It's short, simple, and says something about what I sell.

If you want to sell trains and your name is Dan, you could try danstrains.

If your name is Mona, and your reason for selling on eBay is to get some cash for Christmas presents, you could try: monaschristmascash.

If you can't come up with a good idea right now, don't sweat it. eBay lets you change your id every 30 days.

***

PayPal account. You're also going to need a way to get paid. PayPal is the simplest and most popular payment method on eBay. If you don't have a PayPal account, you can get one by visiting sign up for PayPal.

When you go to sign up, they're going to ask you if you want a personal account, or a business account. The choice is entirely up to you. If you go with the personal account, and later decide eBay selling is really your thing, you can upgrade to a business account then.

The really great thing about PayPal is, as soon as your customer pays them, PayPal pays you. One option I would recommend is a PayPal debit card. With it you have access to your money immediately. Transferring money to your bank account can take 3 to 5 days.

eBay also allows several other payment methods.

Buyers are allowed to pay by snail mail sending, you a check or money order. However, sellers are not allowed to say that they will accept checks or money orders in their item listings. If a buyer asks if they can send cash, check, or money order – it is ok for you to let them.

Sellers can also accept Propay, Skrill, Paymate, and credit card processing through your own merchant service provider. If you offer local pickup for your items, sellers are allowed to pay when picking up their item.

***

A few other things that will make this whole thing easier are a digital camera or scanner, depending upon the type of item you are selling. Your cell phone camera will also work just fine.

A ruler will also come in handy. Don't worry. We're not going to take any complicated measurements or anything. What the ruler does is add a scale for someone to help them picture the size of your item. In these days of close-up photography it's often hard to imagine how big something is. A ruler with large numbers makes it real easy for buyers to see what they are buying. You can say 6 inches, but a picture often says it better. Many people understand visuals much easier.

I've also seen this done well with a twenty dollar bill. Everyone is familiar with the size of money. Set a cool twenty dollar bill alongside of your item and the size question is answered.

***

And, finally, before you get started, you will want to find a nice quiet spot to work in.

What should you sell?

One of the hardest things for most people is figuring out what they want to sell on eBay.

It doesn't have to be that hard. Most people get started on eBay by selling items that they have around the house. Look around you. You probably have great things scattered all over the house that you are no longer using.

Do you have some shoes you never wear anymore, but still look great? Have you upgraded your old cell phone in the past year? If you have kids, did they outgrow any of their clothes? Remember that ugly sweater mom gave you for Christmas last year? Has anyone taken any college classes recently? Someone is going to need those textbooks.

We bought everyone Kindle Fire's last year after Christmas, but one of the kids decided she couldn't live without an I-pad, and now that Kindle just sits there unused. Bet it could fetch a few dollars on eBay?

Do you get the idea? We all have things sitting around the house that we no longer use. They're still great items. And, the chances are pretty good, that there's somebody out there who'd be willing to pay you a few bucks to get them.

The reason most people don't get past this first step is they can't see the value in the things around them. Sure, you no longer use that land line phone, but chances are somebody will. You can drop it in the trash can, take it to Good Will, or maybe, just maybe – you can take a long hard look at it, and see that phone as a good twenty-five bucks towards the hundred dollars you need.

Notice how putting a dollar value on something can make it more attractive?

Let's take another walk around the house with our "money vision" goggles on. What other great items did you miss the first time around.

Take a close look at your stamp collection. Or baseball card collection. Or Hummel figurines. Do you have any duplicates? Or are there any items that no longer fit in with your collection? Often times, collections evolve over time, and you find yourself with a number of pieces that no longer really fit in with your current collection. With stamps and baseball cards, people often upgrade their collections over time. You start off with a filler card, and as you can afford it, or as you find better ones, you swap it out for a higher grade card. The good news is – you're not the only one who does this. Lots of other collectors do the same thing. That bumpy edged, creased Hank Aaron card may be just what they're looking for to complete a 1955 Topps set.

Does anyone in your house play video games? Most homes today have three or four video games systems, many of which are no longer used. Take a few minutes to look for games you haven't played in a while. Chances are someone on eBay is looking for those games, or game systems.

      ***

My dad had this habit of stashing all of our old toys, comic books, and such in the rafters of the garage. If I remember correctly we had Match Box cars, baseball cards, G I Joes, Rock Em Sock Em Robots, and lots of other cool stuff. Might be worth a trip to visit the parents, don't you think?

A quick glance at eBay shows Rock Em Sock Em Robots in the box at $187.25, with 13 bids, and 14 hours to go. Somebody's going to have a nice payday!

      ***

Now I know there are going to be a few sour pusses out there who say they "got nothing." Like Charlie Brown at Halloween, they've got a bag full of rocks.

Suppose there really is nothing in your house that you can sell. How are you going to get that $100 you need?

For some people, it can be as easy as going to the store. Several Christmases ago my wife was shopping at Jo Ann Fabrics and came across Bedazzler's discounted to five bucks. She had been looking at them on eBay, and they were selling for $80 to $100, so when she got home the first thing she did was check eBay again. Still $80 to $100. She compared her Bedazzler to those that were selling on eBay, and sure enough – they were the same. The eBay sellers didn't have any "magic bedazzler's," they were just getting a whole lot more money for the ones they had.

To make a long story short, we bought every Bedazzler that Jo Ann Fabric had, as well as all of the ones available from every JoAnn's within fifty miles.

I sold 87 Bedazzler's for $50 to $75 over a six week period. I probably could have gotten more money for them, but I unloaded them too quickly and flooded the market.

I like old books. Every now and then I will visit used bookstores in town looking for new items I can sell. Last summer I discovered three county history books from the late 1800's. I got them for $100 to $125 each. With-in two weeks, I sold them all on eBay for $250 to $400 each.

If you ever go to estate sales they have loads of great stuff waiting for you to discover. Local auctions offer the same opportunity. Remember to put your "money vision" goggles on when you visit these places. You will be amazed at all of the great things you've been walking by for your entire life.

As you've seen, it doesn't take a lot of time or effort to find things to sell. You just have to really look at the things around you. Profitable items are everywhere.

***

Now that we've all picked out what we're going to sell, the next section is going to go into the nitty-gritty of how to sell them. This is important to you because eBay has millions of sellers, and they are all competing with you to get the buyers attention.

Luckily for you, most sellers have no idea what they have, or how to sell it.

eBay Selling 101

Let me repeat what I said in the last chapter.

> *Most sellers have no idea what they have, or how to sell it …*

What's the secret to selling your item for the most money possible?

It's easy…

Put yourself in your buyer's shoes. Take a minute to really think about why they want what you're selling. Who is the ideal customer for it? Why would anyone want your old Kindle? What can they do with it? What could they do with it? Most people never think of using it for more than reading. Did you?

My suggestion is to think of all of the ways an item can be used, and pick out five or six of them to sell your buyer on.

In the case of the Kindle, obviously you can use it to read e-books. Most sellers are going to leave it at that. It's easy. They don't have to put a whole lot of thought into it. Shoot a picture. Say I've got a Kindle Fire. Give me a hundred bucks.

Unfortunately, if you do the same thing, your poor Kindle Fire is going to be lost in the crowd. A quick search shows 1208 of them on sale today.

Let's try to up the odds of selling our Kindle. What if we said our Kindle was also a great internet tablet. And, now that I think of it, my youngest daughter is always downloading movies and TV shows to watch on it. It's great for email, and oh yeah! With a USB cord, you can move your documents over to it. And, did I mention, you can also download music, and listen to it with your ear-buds. Maybe we could say it's the poor man's I-pad?

It doesn't really matter what you're selling. You need to think out of the box when you're listing items on eBay.

Like I mentioned earlier, my thing is old books and magazines. Every day old volumes of Harper's Magazine from the 1850's to the early 1900's come up for sale on eBay. They sell for $10 to $15. The majority of sellers pop up a picture of the dilapidated old leather cover falling apart from age, and say it's an old book in poor condition. Very few of them open the book to look at all the great woodcut illustrations. Why not show a few of these? Perhaps it would help to list some of the contents? It will take some extra time, but the odds are the time you spend attending to these details can be the difference between selling your book for $10 or for $50.

Let me give you an example.

There is a book seller that I've been following on eBay for five or six years now. He sells the same books that everyone else sells for $10 to $25. The only difference is he receives dozens of bids on his, and often sells the exact same book for $100 to $200.

Any guesses why he receives so much more money for his books? He puts in the extra time to craft a great description. He tells people what the book is about. He shares passages from it. And, he isn't stingy with pictures. Many of his listings have twenty or more pictures in them. Sure, you can say a book has great illustrations. But, a picture will show buyers exactly how great those illustrations are.

With all that being said, what's the perfect description?

What I suggest is you write the best description you can for each item. Don't worry about how long it takes. Worry about what potential buyers need to know.

The first thing you need to know is selling on eBay isn't free. It's going to cost you a little money. The nice thing about eBay is you don't have to pay your fees when you list your item. Normally they bill you about thirty days later. This gives you plenty of time to sell your item, and collect your payment, before you pay eBay.

As an eBay member without an eBay Store, eBay gives you an extra bonus for selling.

> *Your first fifty auction style listings are FREE. You can also add Buy-it-Now to those listings for free. You only have to pay final value fees if your item sells.*

Used properly, and combined with your great items, this should be more than enough opportunities to make some extra cash.

About eBay fees. Depending upon what you are selling, eBay is going to hit you with an 8% to 15% final value fee when your item sells. It's part of the cost of doing business. Consider it your rent. If you have a store, you have to pay the landlord. If you list your stuff in the paper you have to pay for the ad. If you sell at a flea market you have to pay for your booth. eBay is no different. You have to pay to play.

eBay is the place where everybody gathers to checkout, and buy, other people's junk. If you're not there, you're not going to see that hundred bucks you need.

Different Ways to Sell

If you're not familiar with eBay, there are several different ways to list your items for sale. The three main types of listings are: 1) Auction, 2) Fixed Price, and 3) Classified Listings.

Of the three, auction and fixed price are what you will be using most.

Auction listing, allows potential buyers to bid against each other for your item, much as they would by attending a local auction. The way it works is – bidders place what is called a "proxy bid." When they do this they tell eBay that they are willing to spend up to a certain amount, $10.00, $15.00, whatever they set as their upper bid limit. From here eBay places your bid for you up to your maximum bid. If the seller starts her auction at $9.99, and your "proxy bid" is $25.00, ebay will place your bid for $9.99, the seller's minimum acceptable bid. If someone else places a bid, they will advance yours, up to your $25.00 limit.

Fixed price listings are much like walking into your local Wal-Mart or Best Buy. You see a price on the shelf, and that is the price you have to pay. There is no bargaining, finagling, or whatever. Whoever agrees to pay the asking price gets the item.

Classified Listings are more informational. They are a way for businesses to get information out there about what they are doing. An example would be someone selling eBay training seminars. They can give information about their offering, and give you an email address or phone number to follow up with for more information (something not allowed in auction or fixed price listings).

eBay also offers variations on the above listings that everyone should consider using. The most important of these tools is **Buy-It-Now**. By adding buy-it-now to your auction listing you have the ability to start your item at a low price, yet reach for the sky. If someone exercises the buy-it-now option, the auction ends, and the bidder wins the item. If on the other hand, someone makes the minimum bid, the buy-it-now option disappears, and the only way to buy the item is by bidding on it.

The way I use buy-it-now is to set my starting price at the lowest price I am willing to accept. Then I set my buy-it-now price at three or four times my starting price. It's the price I would ideally like to receive.

Best offer is another spin that eBay offers for fixed price auctions. Best offer is just like it sounds. You price the item, and potential buyers can buy your item at the fixed price, or they can send you an offer. Be prepared to laugh a little, and cry a little, at some of the offers you are going to receive. I had a guy one day who made a $1.00 offer on fifty different items that I was selling for $25.00 each. You would think he would have better things to spend his time on.

What I've found is the majority of people are going to offer you between one-half and two-thirds of your asking price. Some of them will continuously low-ball you at $5.00, and others will thank-you profusely for just taking a few bucks off the price.

The good news is: eBay lets you totally automate the process. When you set up the best offer option you can tell eBay to accept all offers over such and such a price, and to automatically decline all offers below a certain price. This way you will never see any of those low-ball offers. The only offers eBay will send to you are the ones that come in between your decline price and your accept price, so that you can manually decide on them.

For example, if I set my accept price at $17.00, and my decline price at $10.00, eBay will accept all offers I receive over $17.00. If an offer comes in under $10.00, they don't bother me with it. It someone makes an offer between $10.00 and $17.00, they send a message to the person making an offer that the seller "is considering their offer." Then it's up to me. I can accept their offer. I can send a counter offer ("Hey - $10.00 is too low, but I would take $15.00"). And, we can bargain back and forth like this for another three tries.

Types of eBay listings

*Auction

1) duration 1 to 7 days – can extend to 10 days for additional 40 cents
2) fees run from 10 cents to $2.00 per listing
3) eBay sellers without stores receive 50 free auctions style listings per month
4) best for unique or one of a kind auctions, or high volume categories such as personal electronics

*fixed price

1) 30 day duration
2) fees vary from 3 cents to 20 cents per listing. Fees for sellers without an eBay store are 50 cents per month
3) best for slow moving items, items with very few potential buyers, or commodity items

*Classified listings

1) 30 day duration
2) fee $9.95 per listing
3) best for informational listings, e-books, and where sellers want to include their phone number website, or email address in listing

Your first listing

This section is going to show you everything you need to know to make your first sale on eBay. When you are done you will know how to write a compelling title that will bring hundreds of potential buyers to your listing, how to write a description that will leave them drooling for more, and how to shoot pictures that sell.

To get started selling you click **sell** at the top of the eBay page, or visit the Tell us what you want to sell page.

If your item has a UPC or ISBN enter it when you are prompted. If you don't have one of these or if you have a unique item select browse categories. This will let you choose a category to list your item in. If you have an older book without an ISBN, select fiction or non-fiction, then drill down into the category that best describes your book. If you're selling a woman's leather jacket, select *women's clothing >> coats and jackets*.

How to write a compelling title

eBay gives you 88 characters to describe your item. The more information you can put into it, the more people are going to see your item.

Why? Because different things are important to different people. Some people are going to search for just IPod, others will search for IPod 8 GB. Still others will be more interested in "certified," others for "Apple certified." If you want to buy on the cheap, but still get something good, you may want "refurbished."

Let's look at a few titles currently listed on eBay for the IPod Touch...

.Apple IPod Touch 4th Generation Black 8GB (Used)

.Apple IPod Touch 32 GB Black (4th Generation) Apple Certified Refurbished

.Great Condition!!! No reserve. Apple IPod Touch 4th Generation Black 32 GB

.Apple IPod Touch 4th Generation 8GB –MC55OLL- works great-camera-earphone

.Apple iPod Touch 4th Generation 16GB New in Factory Sealed Box

Ok. Let's take a close look at those titles.

They're all loaded with keyword rich details.

.8GB, 16 GB, 32 GB

.black / white

.3rd generation / 4th generation

.Apple IPod Touch

.IPod touch

.factory sealed in box

. Apple Certified Refurbished

.camera

.earphone

Are you starting to get the idea?

Yeah! It's an IPod, but that's really the smallest part of it. It's all in the details. What people really want is an IPod

Touch with one or all of the above features. If you're title doesn't include the keywords a buyer is looking for, he is going to move on to the next listing.

Your job is to get them to stop, and make them take a look at your listing.

Let's look at another item

Nike Shoes.

If you type "Nike men's shoes" in the eBay search box, there are 219,158 pairs listed. That's like getting caught in rush hour traffic on the Eisenhower. Your shoes aren't going anywhere.

Without more details your poor shoes are going to be lost in the rush.

What we need to do is level the playing field. You have to think about what's important to people when they're looking for a new pair of shoes.

Some of the things they're going to look for are:

.size

.color (athletic, loafer, dress, work boot)

.width (d, ee)

.model number

.new / used

.new in box

.easy returns

.men's / women's / children's

How many of these terms describe the shoes you are selling? If you want to sell those shoes, you need to fit as many of these keywords as you can in the 88 characters eBay allows you for a title. If you miss just one, you will reduce your chances of making a sale.

A search on the following keywords (men's Nikes 10 ee new in box) reduced the number of pairs shown from 219,158 to six.

Obviously you have a better chance of selling those shoes when you're one of six pairs, rather than one of several hundred thousand.

Remember your title doesn't have to be a complete sentence. It doesn't even have to make sense when you read it. It just needs to have enough keywords in it, so that people can easily find your item.

The takeaway here is to laser focus your title. If you're not sure what keywords should be in your title, search eBay to see which keywords other sellers are using. Or, you can search the manufacturers selling page.

Picture it sold...

You've heard the saying "a picture is worth a thousand words." On eBay you can often times say a picture is worth a thousand dollars.

You can have the best title, a great description, and a killer price, but if your pictures suck you're not likely to make a deal.

When people are ready to buy something, especially expensive items, they demand great pictures. The best example you can find here is your local car dealer. They don't stop with one picture. Most often you will find twenty to twenty-five pictures for every car they are selling. Your car dealer knows most customers shop on the internet before they come in.

As a result dealers give you a virtual tour of the car with the pictures they take. On the outside, they show you front, back, and both sides. There is at least one picture of the engine, a view into the trunk, the upper dash board, the odometer showing the mileage, the floor – front and back, and close ups of any damage.

You can learn a lot about the type of pictures you need by studying car dealers listings. The lighting is always perfect.

Every picture is perfectly centered. They never put in a bad picture. They know that one bad picture can kill the whole deal.

Plan your pictures the same way. You want at least one overall view of your item. You also want close up detailed pictures of any designs. If there is damage – don't just say it in the description make sure to include one or two pictures of the afflicted area. Let potential buyers decide for themselves how bad the damage is.

eBay lets you upload 12 free pictures with every listing. Include as many as you need to tell your story.

***

Beginning in January 2013, eBay is requiring all photos to be a least 500 pixels on the longest end. 1600 pixels is suggested for the best results. I size my pictures at 1000 pixels on the longest end. 1600 pixels makes for too large of a picture file to work with.

How do you resize your pictures?

If you are just running a few auctions, you can manually resize them in MS Paint. Just import your pictures in, use the resize tool, and resave them. In my case, I normally scan 150 to 200 pictures a day and resizing them all manually would probably drive me over the edge. I use Adobe LightRoom. With it I can import all of my pictures with the click of a button, optimize them with two or three mouse clicks, and export them back to my desktop, all in less than five minutes.

Your takeaway here is to get as many pictures as you need to sell your item. If the lighting is off or the picture is off center, man up, and retake it. A few extra minutes redoing it will pay large dividends when you make the sale.

How to craft a great description

We've already touched on the basics of a good description earlier in this book.

This is your sales pitch. The more useful information you can share about your item, the better your chances of selling it at a premium price. Now is the chance to expand on all of those keywords you used in your title.

First and foremost, you need to be honest.

While you are writing about all of the great features your item has, you also need to mention any defects. The last thing you want to do is make a sale, and have it blow up in your face, because of a scratch, or any other minor defect. The truth is most people aren't worried about minor flaws or defects as long as they know about them when they are making the purchase. What bothers people is finding out about any problems after they've laid down their hard earned money.

What makes a great description ...

Let's look at a few, and you will get a better idea how to craft a winning description every time.

***

Up for auction is a rare U.S. Senate document of Dubuque, Iowa historical interest, a March 30, 1846 report, 26 pages long, detailing the findings of the Committee on Private Land Claims regarding the claims of Julien Dubuque and August Chouteau and their heirs to "a tract of one hundred and forty-eight thousand… arpens of land, situate on the river Mississippi, at a place called the Spanish Mines, about four hundred and forty miles from St. Louis." After the Louisiana Purchase, the U.S. government had to determine the validity of various French and Spanish land claims. In the document, the history of Dubuque and Chouteau's claim to the land, including their purchase of the land from the "Sac and Fox nation of Indians" in 1788. Detailed discussion within about the validity of the claim, about the validity of the sale by the tribes, and much more. Today, this area contains the city of Dubuque, Iowa. A fascinating document. Originally bound into a larger bound volume of Senate reports, but discovered as such, and in total, a self-contained work of its own. Binding still holding. Quite rare. Good luck!

***

This auction is for a like new condition Field Gear thick supple leather with super soft Genuine Raccoon Tail. Zip, removable hood. Jacket parka tag size missing but fits like a man's large or extra-large, please see measurements to determine best fit. This jacket is great, with no flaws and looks barely worn! This jacket would make a great gift, or wear it yourself and impress your friends and family. Get this jacket in time for the upcoming fall and winter to look good and stay warm! Make this yours now, and please check out my store.

Measures shoulder to shoulder 21 inches, pit to pit 25 inches, top of shoulder to bottom 33 inches, top of cuff to top of shoulder 24 inches.

***

It is that time of year again. Winter time. We are now starting to bring out our high end winter clothing. We have over 300 pieces of Northface, Spyder, Pendleton, Patagonia and lots of other high end clothing. Be sure to keep on checking back, because we will be putting up a lot of things in the next three months. I also have a lot of winter boots available.

Up for sale is a men's Columbia heavy duty jacket in size XL. Great anorak pull over jacket. Full side zipper. Super good looking and warm. If you know quality, then you know Columbia is the finest clothing out there. This is the same brand that my family wears. Super high end and expensive. You will look fantastic in this clothing. It will keep you warm and dry.

***

Are you beginning to see a pattern?

Each seller is telling a story, and building value in their items. The first one on the document tells you in a short concise description what you can expect to find in it, why it is important, and what condition it is in.

The two clothing items build on emotion. "This is same brand my family wears." "Impress your friends and family." "You will look fantastic in this clothing."

The first clothing item also gives you exact measurements. That way there is no guessing. Anyone who orders can be sure that the coat will fit them.

Another takeaway from the last item is the pitch to look at their other items. "Be sure to keep checking back...I also have a lot of winter boots available."

When you start writing your descriptions refer back to these listings. You want to include specific details about the item you are selling – size, color, brand, and any defects. If you can appeal to any emotions, "look great," "feel good," "be the envy of your friends and neighbors." People are drawn to items they like, but any car salesman can tell you – emotion closes more sales, than anything else.

And, finally, if you are selling complimentary products, for example, jackets and pants, or a series of books or movies – ask your buyers to check out your other auctions.

How to price your items to sell...

Congratulations. You've done it.

You've written a killer title, loaded with keywords. Your description has left them drooling over your item. It tells everything a buyer needs to make an informed decision, and it appeals to their emotions

Now all you've got to do is price it right.

More sales are lost at this step, than anywhere else in the sales process. Too often sellers become overly attached to their items. Especially if it is an item they've owned since childhood, or one with a family history.

You see it on every episode of Pawn Stars. Rick or Cory call in an expert to appraise an item, and the expert appraises it at $1000. Yet the owner stubbornly holds on to their idea that because the item is old, or has sentimental value, or they have this much money into it, that they need a certain price for it, often times $500 or $1000 more than the expert appraised it at.

Bad idea. An item is only worth what someone is willing to pay for it.

Sometimes this fact works in your favor, other times you have to shrug your shoulders, and take what you can get.

In my case, I sell old magazine articles that have no set value. There is no official price so I've learned to wing it, and set my prices by experimenting with where they sell best. I know from past experience what topics are going to sell for more money, or sell quicker. On those items, I jump my price twenty or thirty dollars, and many times I can get it. If they don't sell, I drop the price, and take what I can get.

A lot of items don't allow you this luxury. They sell day in and day out in a very narrow price range, and if you jump out of that price range – No sale.

　　　　***

Here's one of the best ways to set your price to assure a quick sell through, especially if you are a new seller.

You can do a completed item search on eBay using the advanced search feature.

To do a completed item search, find the search box at the top of the eBay page. To the right of the words **SEARCH** it will say **ADVANCED**. Click on **ADVANCED**, and it will take you to another set of search options.

Enter the keywords you want to search on. You can choose to search in just one category, or search listings in all categories (I would recommend this one). A little further down where it says **search including** be sure to check off by **completed listings**. As you scroll down you will see there are a lot more options you can search by. Unless you are looking for some really specialized information the only other two selections I would consider are Auction and Buy It Now under the Selling Formats category.

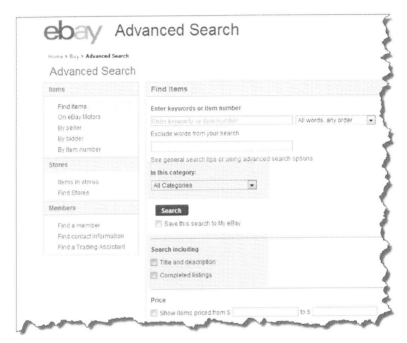

A quick look through completed listings for the last week will give you a good idea of the price range your item has sold in. You can drill down even more by clicking on the listings that sold for the most money and garnered the most bids.

Take a close look at the keywords they used in the title, what they said in the description, the type and number of pictures they included, and finally look at what price they started their listing at. No use reinventing the wheel, write all of this down and you can include much of it when you go to post your own listings.

This way you can see exactly what items like yours have sold for. If enough items have sold, you will have a very good idea how much money your item should sell for.

There are several pricing theories.

One holds that you should price every item at 99 cents and let the market set the price. This works well with items that sell in large quantities and normally sell within a tight price range. Electronics are a good example where this strategy can work for you. There are always plenty of buyers ready to pounce on an Ipad, Iphone, or laptop. Starting your item at 1 cent or 99 cents is normally going to spark a bidding war and bring you the best possible price.

Other people prefer knowing that their item is going to bring at least a certain price. If you're selling an item that normally brings $100 to $125, maybe you can price it at $85, and throw in a Buy-It-Now option for $125. This guarantees at least a minimum price if your item sells, while giving you a shot at getting the best price if someone exercises your Buy-It-Now.

Whatever you do, think really hard on using the 99 cent strategy if you are selling a collectible or one of a kind item. Often times a collectible, no matter how rare, only has one buyer at any given time. If you can't spark a bidding war that $100 or $500 item could end up selling for 99 cents.

Talk about bringing out the Christmas Scrooge. That would give you the bah hum-bugs for quite some time to come.

Shipping your item

The biggest thing to keep in mind about shipping is: You are responsible for the item until the seller receives it.

If it gets lost in the mail, you need to make good on it. If it arrives damaged, you need to make good on it. If your shipment arrives incomplete, and the buyer says all the pieces aren't there, you need to make good on it.

Do you see a pattern developing here?

You need to package your item properly. If you're selling plates, glassware or other fragile items, you need to pack them so they arrive undamaged. If you're mailing photos or items that can be easily bent or folded, you need to package them in a sturdy mailer, and mark "Do not bend, or fold" all over the package. I don't know about your mail person, but my mail lady likes to bend and fold everything so she can cram it all in that tiny mail box.

Take a few moments before you list any item to think about how you are going to mail it. Will your item fit in a small box or card stock mailer? Or are you going to require lots of elaborate packing materials and sturdy corrugated boxes? The item you are selling is going to affect how you need to ship your item, and what you are going to charge for shipping.

eBay allows you several ways to charge shipping fees. You can choose flat rate, where everyone pays the same shipping charge no matter where they live. With this method if you set your shipping fee at $5.00 everyone would pay $5.00, whether they live in the same state as you, or 2000 miles away in Alaska or Hawaii. You can also choose "calculated shipping." With calculated shipping you enter the weight of your item when you list it, and eBay automatically calculates shipping charges to any destination. By using calculated shipping, someone living closer to you normally pays less for shipping, making your item more attractive to them.

eBay also lets you choose several methods of shipping. Among the choices you can offer are first class, media mail, priority mail, or express mail. By offering choices buyers can elect a less expensive method of shipping, or chose a more expensive method that will get their item to them quicker.

One other obstacle you're going to bump up against is Free Shipping. eBay suggests that everyone should offer free shipping. They think you should absorb shipping and handling fees into your pricing. My suggestion is to see what other sellers are doing with similar items. If everyone else is offering free shipping you should probably join the pack. Otherwise I would suggest charging separately for shipping.

***

eBay makes it easy for you to mail items.

You can print shipping labels directly from the item listing as soon as your buyer pays. To do this click **My eBay** at the top of the eBay page. Select **Sold** items in your selling manager. From here you can just go to the item you need to mail and click in the final column where it says sell similar. From the drop down menu select **print shipping labels**. From here you will be taken to the Print a shipping label page.

After this fill in the weight and shipping method if they aren't already prepopulated for you. From there it's just a simple matter of selecting the options you want. You can add delivery confirmation, signature confirmation, and insurance.

I want to take a minute and define those last three terms:

Delivery confirmation means that the mailman scans your package when he leaves it at your customer's house. It is proof that your item was delivered. If you print your mailing label through eBay or PayPal, delivery confirmation is included with most options. If you mail your item at the Post Office you need to fill out a special form, and pay the fee (55 cents at this writing).

You want to include delivery confirmation with every item you sell. It keeps you and your buyer honest. The first thing eBay or PayPal are going to do if the buyer starts an item not delivered case is check delivery confirmation. If it shows delivered – you win. If there's no delivery confirmation, you pretty much lose because there is no way to prove your item was ever shipped, let alone delivered.

Signature confirmation is similar to delivery confirmation, except the buyer has to sign for your package in order to receive it. eBay and PayPal require signature confirmation on orders valued at over $200. You can include it with the label you print on line (the fee is $2.00). Once again, if you do your shipping at the Post Office you will need to fill out a separate form there.

Insurance is an extra you can add to most packages. Insurance pays for damage or loss of your items while in transit. You don't have to purchase insurance. It is an option. What you do need to remember is: The seller is responsible for an item until it is delivered to the buyer in the condition you offered it for sale. If the item does not arrive, or arrives damaged, you are responsible.

Another thing to remember is eBay does not allow sellers to charge buyers for insurance. You can build it into your shipping cost, or into the price of your item. You cannot charge for it as a standalone option.

Your take away here is to carefully pack and ship every item you sell. Select the shipping options and extras that are important to you. If you decide not to insure every package, pick a price point $50 or $100 that you will buy insurance at and stick to that. This way you can somewhat limit your losses in case something unfortunate happens.

Customer Service is everything

On eBay the only thing a seller has is their good reputation.

Every time you sell an item the buyer has the opportunity to leave a feedback rating on how well they thought you handled the transaction. First they can leave a written comment on what they thought of your service and product. Buyers can also rate you in four categories including: item description, communication, how quickly you shipped their item, and cost of shipping.

It's called a five star rating system because they can give you from one to five stars in each category.

You would think getting four stars would be great. And it would in an ideal system, but in the eBay world four out of five stars can get you thrown off the site for poor customer service. eBay considers 4.8 to 5.0 as excellent customer service. Anything below 4.6 is considered unsatisfactory and you can lose your selling privileges.

So how do you give good customer service on eBay?

It all starts with your listing. You need to accurately describe all of your items. If there are any flaws you need to be sure to describe them completely, and add photographs where possible.

Don't overcharge for shipping. Shipping charges are a really touchy issue on eBay right now. Even a hint of overcharging your customers can draw negative feedback in all four categories.

Answer your email. If someone asks questions before or after the sale, respond immediately.

Respond to complaints immediately. Apologize profusely. Accept all blame for the problem, even if it's clear you're not at fault. When someone writes me because they have not received their item yet, even if they just paid two days ago and its shipping to Japan, I start my email with:

"I'm sorry to hear that you have not received your item yet. I did check my records. Your payment was received on ----, and it was mailed on ---. Normal delivery time is ------, so you should receive your item soon. Please keep me advised. Nick"

Notice – I didn't go off on them for expecting the impossible. I apologized. I told them the facts – when they paid, and when their item was mailed. And finally, I set expectations for delivery time. And, I ended with telling them it's ok to keep in touch.

Show concern. That's really all most people want.

What about requests for refunds? One of my first jobs was with Radio Shack, and every time we had to give out a refund the manager would head for the back room as soon as the customer left and start screaming and ranting. Often times he would smash the returned item crashing it into the wall or the floor. I mention this only to point out how not to handle the situation.

When you're selling on line and someone wants a refund, your reputation is at stake. The best thing you can do is apologize. Offer a full refund, including shipping both ways. The only alternative is facing the likelihood of receiving negative feedback. In the long run that's going to cost you more than any refund you can give.

Time to get started...

Ok. We've covered how to find items to sell. How to list your items and how to price them for a quick sale

One final suggestion that may help you is to read through the seller profiles in the back of this book. Basically each of them shares a little bit about their eBay journey – How it started, where they see it going, and how their experiences may help you.

I put my profile first. It's pretty typical of most sellers experiences as they go through the ups and downs of selling on eBay.

I know you can do it. Every day thousands of people just like you are getting started selling on eBay. Thousands more want to give it a try, but are afraid to try. Don't be one of them.

Good luck and great selling.

Nick

Case Studies

Nick – Historical Collectibles

My own story is typical of many eBay sellers.

I got my first taste of on line auctions in 1999. I had been following eBay and Yahoo Auctions for some time, and one day, I decided to take the plunge. I bought a couple baseball cards.

And then I bought some more, and some more. It was like an addiction.

Anyway, one thing led to another, and pretty soon I had this crazy idea that maybe I could sell some baseball cards, too. At this time I was buying "lots" of 1954 and 1955 Topps baseball cards thinking I could piece together a set. Many of the cards were lower grade, with creases and bruised corners, but they were a start.

Whenever I got a better card it went in my set. The other cards ended up in a cast off pile. As time went by I found myself with quite a few of these castoffs. And, they ended up being my first foray into auction selling.

My auctions were pretty unsophisticated at that time. Basically, I would scan a picture of the card, front and back, add a little description, and post it on eBay. Most of them I priced between $1.00 and $5.00 based on how mangled they were.

But the thing is - people bought them. Sometimes I even had bidding wars erupt, where they would jump from $1.00 to $10.00 and even $20.00 occasionally. Pretty cool stuff.

This went on for probably six months, and I was doing ok. I wasn't really making any money, because even though I was selling several hundred dollars-worth of cards a month, I was buying just as much or more. But it felt really good, because people were sending me money. Every day I received cash and checks in the mail, and dutifully I would package those baseball cards up, stuff them in an envelope, and mail them off to their new owners.

It was definitely fun. And to make it more interesting, back in those days, many people sent you cash, so many times, I had ten and twenty dollar bills falling out of all those envelopes.

Then one day I had one of those epiphany moments. I was perusing through the auction listings and caught sight of a guy selling an old magazine article (not a whole magazine, just one article taken from a magazine). It made me stop.

And think. What kind of a nutcase would buy, or sell, a magazine article?

I read his description. I looked at his pictures. He was asking $10.00.

I needed to know a little more. So I looked at the other items he was selling, and he had about fifteen or twenty of these magazine articles for sale. Some of them had bids. A couple of them were over $20.00.

I looked at his sold history. And, over the past six months he had sold nearly one hundred magazine articles. Not bad for a few pieces of paper torn out of a musty old book.

I went back to selling my baseball cards. But over the next few weeks my thoughts kept wandering back to that guy selling magazine articles. I liked history. I liked books. It seemed like something I could do.

My first step into this new venture was to purchase a copy of Harper's Magazine from 1865. It had a good mix of articles. Some articles were on the Civil War and others on historical places and events.

My investment was a whopping $15.00. And, like just about all of the items I sell, I bought it on eBay.

When my issue of Harper's arrived I paged through it. Before I took it apart, I made a list of which articles I was going to sell, how I was going to describe them, and how much I was going to ask for them.

Anyway, to make a long story short, I sold most of those articles pretty quickly. My $15.00 investment quickly turned into $250.00. And like my venture with baseball cards, I found myself buying more and more, and still more books to break apart and sell.

Today I have over 6,000 items listed on eBay, and just over 10,000 on Amazon.

Over the past thirteen years I have completed nearly 30,000 sales as history-bytes on eBay alone. I'm just ending my first year of selling on Amazon, and have racked up close to 200 sales there. It's proving to be a tough nut to crack compared to eBay, but I will make it happen.

***

After being laid off in 2004, I jumped into eBay full time. I went from making $500 a month to $5000 a month.

Before doing this, I read everything written about eBay that I could get my hands on. I had someone design a custom template and eBay store interface for me. I plugged my picture into every auction listing hoping to build trust into my listings. I offered a "100% Money Back Guarantee – No Questions Asked."

I went from having 500 listings in my eBay store to maintaining almost 10,000 items listed for sale at any given time. I was listing 400 items each and every week, and I was mailing out nearly 150 packages every week.

It was more work than having a job. I don't think there was a single week that I clocked under 70 hours. It was a seven day work week.

And this is pretty much true of every full time eBay seller I have ever talked with or read about. It's a 24 / 7 job.

You get hooked on it.

* * *

Many of my best sales came about by accident. Others happened because of deliberate planning, and a whole lot of luck.

In growing my business I took a lot of chances.

I stretched the barrier every chance I could on pricing. Many of the sellers in my category were selling the same items I was selling for a whole lot less. I was asking $25.00 or $30.00, they were asking $5.00 or $10.00 for the same thing. I decided long ago to go for the gusto. My items have always sold better at a higher price.

I found myself trying a lot of new things.

One of my great successes was selling newspapers. I bought every bound volume I could of the Niles Weekly Register. It was one of the first real National newspapers in America. Over time I was able to assemble almost a complete run from 1811 to 1833.

From 1812 to 1815 they contained great accounts of battles and leaders in the War of 1812. I read through every paper, and listed them on eBay one by one. I included excerpts of battlefield accounts in all of my listings. Two of them on the burning of the White House went for about $100 each. Another, from 1811, contained a printing of the Declaration of Independence, side-by-side with Jefferson's notes for it. That one garnered $250.

I even tried bundling with a few of them. Two of our presidents, Thomas Jefferson and John Adams, died on July 4, 1826. Four papers were dedicated to their lives, an account of their deaths, and news of their funerals. These papers sparked some of the hottest bidding any of my auctions ever received. The final price they sold for was over $500.

Another time I was bidding on an 1840's copy of George Catlin's **Letters and Notes**. I lost the bid. It sold for over $500. But another seller emailed me she had a copy she was willing to part with for $200. I jumped on it, and sold the individual pictures for over $3500. It was a nice score, and brought me lots of new customers.

I stumbled across eight bound volumes of the **Annals of Congress** from the 1830's for $10 each. They were filled with news of the battle at the Alamo and Mexican troop movements in Texas. The Mormon exodus from Illinois and Missouri was discussed over and over again, along with many other popular topics of the day. Once again, I was able to sell individual pages about the Alamo and the Mormon's for $100 or more – each.

****

If I could tell sellers anything about eBay, it would be to develop a specialty that no one else is serving, and work it for all its worth.

Many of my customers have been with me since the first days I started selling on eBay. They know I'm always out there searching for new and unique things. And they appreciate that, and keep coming back to see what new articles I've discovered.

Over the years I've sold items to: the White House Historical Society, the Royal Museum in Jamaica, castles and historical societies all over the United States, Europe, Japan, China, Russia, Australia, and more. Hundreds of authors and publishers count on me for information when they are writing books, and illustrating magazine articles and books.

Museums buy illustrations and articles every day to augment their displays.

Probably the most off the wall sale I ever made was an article I found in a 1950's movie star magazine. There was a letter a from a pregnant movie star to her unborn daughter. Fifty years later her daughter saw that article in one of my listings, and purchased a letter from her mom that she had never seen, or even knew existed.

***

In the thirteen years that I've been selling on eBay technology has changed. People's wants and needs have changed. I now have my own website, digitalhistoryproject.com. I'm offering many of my more popular magazine articles as Kindle and Nook Books.

Who knows where your eBay journey will take you?

Jenny was in her first year of college when the eBay bug struck her.

She had always had an artsy side. One of the things that intrigued Jenny about eBay was that it allowed her to build an artist platform that could reach millions of people.

Two of her friends had opened eBay stores where they could showcase their art works. What they liked about eBay was the ability to include an artist biography on their "me" page. Each listing allowed them to expand on their biography, adding more details. They were also able to showcase each work with unlimited illustrations, and to describe the story behind each of their works.

Shortly after this Jenny opened her own store. She hired a professional to design her storefront, and put together a custom template to list her artwork with. She was determined that everything had to be professional from the get-go. Her eBay career began with fifteen listings, all original paintings. She priced them reasonably, anywhere from $250 up to $1500 for her most expensive work, a giant 36" x 60" painting.

Sales were nonexistent the first few months. She can recall checking her sales every few hours the first week waiting for the magic to happen. It didn't. And, as the weeks began to drag into months she began having serious doubts about the whole idea. Her friends had both made sales their first month, and all of the waiting for a sale to happen gave her endless worries.

Several times she lowered her prices $50 and $100 at a time, but still no sales.

And then one day she received an email. It was a lady asking about one of her paintings. She wanted to know a little more about it, and she wanted exact dimensions to see if it would fit into a frame she had. That was an "ah-ha" moment for Jenny. She had given approximate dimensions in her listings, not thinking that people needed exact sizes to fit frames they already had, or a particular space they wanted to display her art in.

After that she decided to take a good look at all of her listings, and ended up making several changes.

Of course she added the actual dimensions of each work. She talked more about the paintings themselves. She explained what she was feeling when she painted them, who her influences were during the period she painted them, the type of brush strokes she used, the subtleness of the colors, and symbolism she used in them.

She also gave suggestions about where they would look good. "A similar painting of mine hangs over the fireplace in a major corporate office." "Another painting in this series is the centerpiece of so-and-so's den." "The colors in this outdoor scene would go great in a rustic cabin setting."

She started including more feedback from people who liked her artwork – "reminiscent of," "made me think of," "the colors seemed to," "When I saw it, all I could think of was."

"I decided to get them thinking about where they could exhibit my paintings," said Jenny. "I wanted to get the internal conversation going, by including some of the emotions my paintings brought out in people looking at them."

Once she did this, customers started engaging her in more email conversations. And, from here she started to make more sales. "It was like people needed a little nudge," Jenny told me. "They wanted to know what my paintings were all about. And they wanted to know more about me both as a person and as an artist."

Another change she made was to add limited edition prints of some of her more popular works. She discovered that people were more apt to jump in and buy her works for $50 or $100, than for $500 or $1000.

***

If Jenny could give other artists any advice, it would be "to be patient. It takes people time to find you on eBay, and it takes them more time to actually take the plunge and buy your works."

"While you're waiting for buyers to come along, make sure your profile is up to date. Write an exciting **me** page, telling about your artworks and any awards you've won. Make it personal and fun."

"Make sure all of your listings really talk up your offering. Include plenty of great quality pictures, and let people know its ok to contact you with questions."

Bill's thing was cars.

You learn that right away when you start talking with him. Everything he says seems to go back to cars. Especially Mustangs. His first one was a 1966 convertible he bought when he was in his early twenties. It was green. Since then he's owned thirteen different Mustangs.

By day he's a corporate lawyer in a large insurance office. But nights and weekends, Bill is all about cars. He has a five car garage and he has three projects going just about all of the time.

Bill's entry into eBay was looking for parts to complete one of his cars. He needed a windshield wiper switch for a '68 Mustang and nobody local had one, so he turned to eBay. He found three of them on eBay, and snapped one up "at a pretty good price."

When he was looking for the wiper switch he discovered eBay had thousands of other Mustang parts, many that he always had trouble finding where he lived. Over the next few months he was drawn back to eBay several times, and was surprised how easy it was to find and buy just about any part he needed.

That got Bill thinking. Over the last twenty years he had filled several sheds with parts he'd taken from projects cars that he stripped down to rebuild others. He did a little reading about how to sell on eBay, and talked with some friends who made occasional sales there.

His first sale was a mirror set for a 1971 Mustang – fifty bucks.

From that point on Bill was entirely jacked up about selling on eBay. Pretty soon he was listing twenty, even thirty parts a week. Many of them were selling at a pretty good price. What really surprised Bill though, was all of the emails people started sending him once they saw how many Mustang parts he was selling. They had to see what other goodies he might have stored away.

Bill soon found himself to be considered a "Mustang expert." Not only were people asking him if he had this or that part, "they were asking me for my advice," he said. "They wanted to know if I knew anything about body work, or how to replace this or that part."

Several times people contacted him to see if he was looking for project cars. Once he found himself traveling from a little town outside of Chicago all of the way to Bangor, Maine for a '65 Mustang he just had to have.

Another time he was offered a 1965 Pony Fastback. That one was in Wisconsin, so he didn't have to go quite so far for it.

According to Bill "the next logical step was to start selling cars." He sold his first one about two years ago – a '71 Mach One that he had completely restored. Since then he's sold three more cars in various stages of restoration.

"I'm finally doing what I always wanted to," says Bill. "Right now, I'm restoring two to three cars a year. eBay gives me a ready market for selling them. I think the longest it took to sell any of them was three weeks. The second one sold the first week."

But, "the best thing," according to Bill is the recognition. Once he joined the conversation, posting on automotive bulletin boards, it wasn't long until he became the "go-to guy" for all things Mustang. He's even written several articles for national magazines.

"Selling on eBay put me out there as an expert," says Bill. "Now I'm not that lawyer with the crazy fetish for cars! I'm 'Mr. Mustang.'"

"See you selling on eBay!" exclaims Bill.

Johnnie – Information products

Johnnie was crippled in a car accident nearly twenty years ago. Since then he's had to use a wheel chair to get around.

"Life hasn't been easy since then," admits Johnnie. "I get disability and there was a settlement from the accident that gave me some money to get by on. It's just that I've always felt sort of useless since it happened.

"I was a construction worker, and it's not like there's much work for a guy in a wheel chair. Not in that line of work anyway." He laughs thinking about Joe Swanson, the "handicapable" cop on **Family Guy** chasing criminals down the street in his wheel chair. If only life was a cartoon.

***

Several years ago Johnnie read an e-book about selling information products on eBay. He bought it and several other e-books, too. Two of them had something called "resell rights" that allowed him to resell the books for himself on eBay or anywhere else he chose.

Johnnie decided it was something he could do.

His first attempts on eBay were really simple. He found some clip art of hundred dollar bills in a money clip, and put them in his listing, along with a few details telling everyone how much money they could make using the e-book system. Unsure what to charge, he decided inexpensive was the way to go. He priced his offering at 97 cents.

The first month Johnnie sold 33 copies of that e-book. He didn't make a whole lot of money after paying eBay, but he did see the potential.

Before long, Johnnie had an eBay store stocked with over two hundred e-books. At 97 cents each he was selling close to 500 e-books. That was still a long way from where he wanted to be. Johnnie decided there were only two ways he could grow his e-book business: 1) Sell more books, and 2) Charge more money.

His first move was to selectively raise prices. By this time several of his e-books had sold 100 copies or more. On each of these he raised his price to $5.99. All of the other books he re-priced between $2.99 and $4.99. He even featured five books at $19.99. For these five books, he made all new covers, and he rewrote the descriptions from the ground up.

The results surprised even Johnnie. "I still sold 400 books the month after I raised all those prices. I'd always thought a low price was the only reason people bought my e-books," said Johnnie. "I never really gave a thought to it until then. They were looking for the solutions my books brought them. They weren't thinking about the price!"

And, about those books he priced at $19.99. "I sold seven of them that first month," added Johnnie. "Seven!"

    ***

Today, he's still going strong on eBay. But now Johnnie is writing his own e-books, and next week he's going to publish his first Kindle e-book. "Gotta keep up," he says.

Good luck, and great selling.

If you are happy with the information in this book, please visit the books page on Amazon, and leave a review. Your honest advice will be appreciated by all potential readers. As with anything, the more good reviews, the more people will be interested in looking at the book.

If you have any comments or questions, you can contact me at nick@digitalhistoryproject.com.

22971420R00044

Made in the USA
Lexington, KY
22 May 2013